Children of the World
El Salvador

For a free color catalog describing Gareth Stevens' list of high-quality children's books, call 1-800-341-3569 (USA) or 1-800-461-9120 (Canada).

For their help in the preparation of *Children of the World: El Salvador*, the editors gratefully thank Professor Michael Fleet, Marquette University, Milwaukee, and Luisa Sandoval.

Library of Congress Cataloging-in-Publication Data

Cummins, Ronnie.
      El Salvador / written by Ronald Cummins; photography by Rose Welch.
         p. cm. — (Children of the world)
      Summary: Presents the life of a twelve-year-old boy and his family in El Salvador, describing his home and school activities and discussing the history, geography, ethnic composition, natural resources, languages, government, religions, culture, and economics of his country.
      ISBN 0-8368-0220-9
      1. El Salvador—Social life and customs—Juvenile literature. 2. Children—El Salvador—Juvenile literature. [1. Family life—El Salvador. 2. El Salvador.] I. Welch, Rose, ill. II. Title. III. Series: Children of the world (Milwaukee, Wis.)
F1483.8.C86   1990
972.84—dc20   89-43137

A Gareth Stevens Children's Books edition
Edited, designed, and produced by

Gareth Stevens Children's Books
RiverCenter Building, Suite 201
1555 North RiverCenter Drive
Milwaukee, Wisconsin 53212, USA

Series editor: Valerie Weber
Editor: Amy Bauman
Research editor: Mary Jo Baertschy
Designer: Laurie Shock
Map design: Sheri Gibbs

Printed in the United States of America

1 2 3 4 5 6 7 8 9 96 95 94 93 92 91 90

Children of the World
El Salvador

Text by Ronnie Cummins
Photographs by Rose Welch

Gareth Stevens Children's Books
MILWAUKEE

. . . a note about *Children of the World*:

The children of the world live in fishing towns, Arctic regions, and urban centers, on islands and in mountain valleys, on sheep ranches and fruit farms. This series follows one child in each country through the pattern of his or her life. Candid photographs show the children with their families, at school, at play, and in their communities. The text describes the dreams of the children and, often through their own words, tells how they see themselves and their lives.

Each book also explores events that are unique to the country in which the child lives, including festivals, religious ceremonies, and national holidays. The *Children of the World* series does more than tell about foreign countries. It introduces the children of each country and shows readers what it is like to be a child in that country.

Children of the World includes the following published and soon-to-be-published titles:

Australia	El Salvador	Japan	Spain
Bhutan	England	Jordan	Sweden
Bolivia	Finland	Malaysia	Tanzania
Brazil	France	Mexico	Thailand
Burkina Faso	Greece	Nepal	Turkey
Burma	Guatemala	New Zealand	USSR
China	Hong Kong	Nicaragua	Vietnam
Costa Rica	Hungary	Philippines	West Germany
Cuba	India	Singapore	Yugoslavia
Czechoslovakia	Indonesia	South Africa	Zambia
Egypt	Italy	South Korea	

. . . and about *El Salvador*:

Twelve-year-old Andrés Navarro Aquino comes from a family of nine children. He was born and raised on a farm in rural El Salvador. Until the country's civil war forced them from the farm, the family managed to carve out an existence, raising mainly corn, beans, and chickens. The Navarros now live in a depressed section of San Salvador, working hard once more and looking — along with many other Salvadorans — to their future.

To enhance this book's value in libraries and classrooms, comprehensive reference sections include up-to-date information about El Salvador's geography, demographics, currency, culture, education, industry, and natural resources. *El Salvador* also features a bibliography, research topics, activity projects, and discussions of such subjects as San Salvador, the country's history, political system, ethnic and religious composition, and language.

The living conditions and experiences of children in El Salvador vary according to economic, environmental, and ethnic circumstances. The reference sections help bring to life for young readers the diversity and richness of the culture and heritage of El Salvador. Of particular interest are discussions of the Spanish conquest of Central America, changes in El Salvador since the civil war began in the 1970s, and the country's situation as the smallest Central American country.

CONTENTS

LIVING IN EL SALVADOR:
Andrés, a Young Artist

Twelve-year-old Andrés Navarro Aquino comes from El Salvador, Central America's smallest country. Andrés, his parents, and his eight brothers and sisters live in a low-income neighborhood, called Oscar Romero, located just outside San Salvador, the capital of El Salvador. Andrés and his family, like many Salvadorans, are victims of a civil war that has been raging between government and rebel troops since the 1970s. The Navarro family used to own a small farm in eastern El Salvador. But when an air force bomb destroyed the farm, they were forced to move to San Salvador.

The main rebel army, called the Farabundo Martí Front for National Liberation (FMLN), claims it is fighting for the needs of the poor masses. The group wants to take over the government and make reforms that it says will force the wealthy minority to share the country's prosperity with the rest of the people. But the government claims that the rebels really want the land and businesses for themselves.

Andrés stands with his family near Lake Ilopango. In the back row (left to right) are Catalina, 45, and Emilio, 46 (Andrés' parents); Daniel, 20; Rafael, 18; and Andrés (in yellow shirt). In the front row are Bartholomé, 8 (in white shirt); Francisco, 11 (in red shirt); Mario, 6; Maria, 4; and Marcos, 9. Dagoberta, Andrés' 13-year-old sister (in the picture at right), did not accompany the family to the lake. Because of the many robberies in the Oscar Romero neighborhood, someone must always stay at home to guard the house.

The capital city, San Salvador, sprawls at the foot of San Salvador Volcano.

From Refugee Camp to City Neighborhood: Andrés' Home

Andrés remembers the day four years ago when air force helicopters attacked the countryside around his family's home. Government soldiers forced the Navarros and their neighbors to move to a camp for war refugees. The family lived in the camp for several years.

When the Navarros moved to San Salvador, they had nowhere to live. Using materials supplied by the local Catholic church, Andrés, his older brothers, and his father, Emilio, built a simple two-room house. Daniel and Rafael taught Andrés to mix cement and to construct a wall using cement blocks. He even helped build the kitchen, which Emilio placed at the back of the house. Placing the kitchen there, Emilio explained, keeps the stove smoke out of the rest of the house. Later, Andrés helped his mother, Catalina, paint the inside walls. As they worked, Andrés told her that he hoped he'd grow up to be as clever as his father.

Opposite, top: The Oscar Romero neighborhood is built on land that was once a garbage dump. The people covered the dump with soil so that houses could be built on it. But because nothing will grow in the thin soil, the streets remain dusty and barren.
Opposite, bottom: Neighborhood children play in the street in front of the Navarros' house, which is painted bright blue.

The poorest of Andrés' neighbors live in shacks made of cardboard, old lumber, and sheets of plastic. None of the houses in the area has an indoor bathroom or running water, but outdoor water faucets stand on several street corners for residents to use. The city government does not supply electricity to the neighborhood either, but the Navarros and many others have hooked up their own electric lines to the public utility lines.

Andrés knows many boys and girls in the community who are his own age. Many of them are war refugees, too. Andrés and his best friend, Manuel, often talk about their lives before they moved to San Salvador. But more often, they talk of the future. Like many boys in the community, Andrés and Manuel worry about being drafted into the army when they are older. Manuel once admitted that he would be afraid to fight. Andrés said that others must also be afraid since many young men have left the country rather than be drafted.

The railroad tracks that run through Oscar Romero pass very close to some of the houses. Vendors sometimes walk up and down the tracks, selling their wares.

Above: In this view of the neighborhood, houses set on the hillside seem to be built on top of one another. The people have used any available material for their buildings.
Right: None of the neighborhood houses has running water. Water must be drawn from one of several faucets found nearby. Here, colorful jugs surround the faucet, waiting to be filled.

Family Life, Past and Present

On their small farm, the Navarros mainly raised corn, beans, and chickens. When not in school, Andrés and the other children worked beside their father in the fields and cared for their small orchard. During harvest time, everyone but the smallest children picked coffee beans on a large plantation in the village. Everyone worked hard, but they always raised enough to eat.

Andrés misses life on the farm. Emilio tells him that if he keeps memories of the farm in his heart, it will always be with him. Emilio understands how Andrés feels. He's been a farmer all his life. He, too, has had a hard time adapting to city life. To earn money last year, he and Rafael rented farmland about 50 miles (80 km) from San Salvador. To tend the land, they had to be away from the family for several months. At harvest time, they were disappointed when their earnings barely covered the rent they had paid on the land.

One of Andrés' pictures shows a man standing near the Navarros' former village. Andrés says that people of his village were happy before the army came and destroyed their homes and fields.

Leaving the farm has not been easy for the Navarros. Above: Andrés uses his drawings as one way to keep the past alive. Many of his pictures show life as it was on the farm.
Below: Beans and corn from last year's harvest on the rented land. Emilio and Rafael's harvest barely covered their rent costs and brought the family little extra food.

15

Even Andrés' youngest brother, Mario, has chores to do. Here, with a pan of corn on his head, he leaves for the neighborhood *molino*, or corn grinder. There, the corn will be ground into the fine powder that is used for making tortillas.

Now that they live in the city, the Navarros still work hard. Although Catalina and Dagoberta do the bulk of the household work, everyone still has chores to do. Francisco and Marcos walk to the neighborhood pump to collect water. Bartholomé carries corn to the *molino*, or grinder, for grinding; Andrés and Daniel collect firewood. Inside the house, Dagoberta and Catalina prepare a breakfast of beans and tortillas while Mario watches little Maria. Andrés jokes that Mario might have the toughest job.

Because buying food, clothes, and other necessities for a family of 11 requires a lot of money, everyone helps in any way he or she can. Emilio and Rafael, discouraged by last year's farming, have been looking for construction jobs in the city. Dagoberta earns money helping a neighbor sell vegetables at the market. Andrés and Daniel have jobs in the carpentry and craft shop that the local church has established.

Catalina makes tortillas from the freshly ground corn for the family's breakfast. Once she begins, she makes the tortillas as quickly as possible. The faster she makes them, the less wood she'll need to burn.

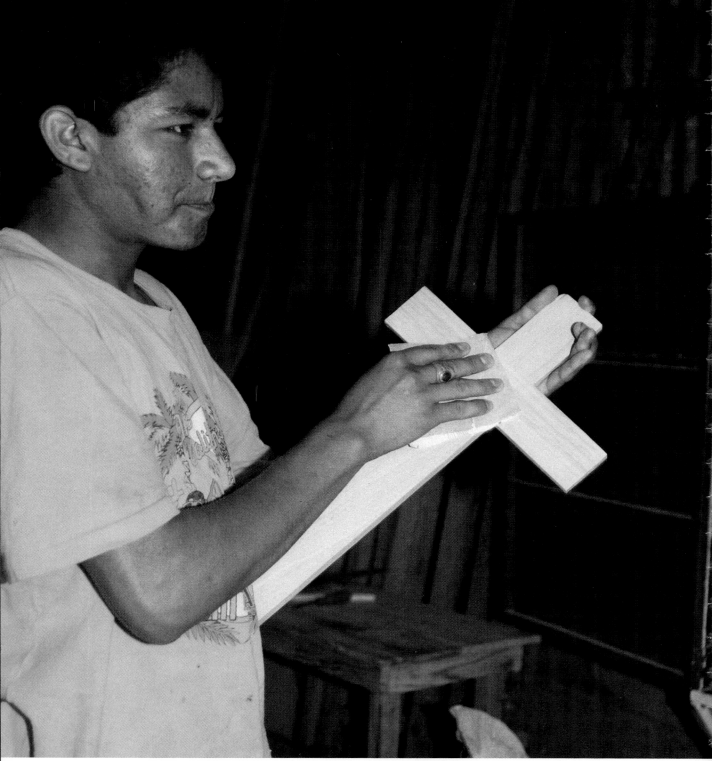

Daniel sands one of the crosses that he has just shaped in the carpentry shop.

The Crafts and Carpentry Cooperative

After breakfast, Andrés and Daniel leave for work at the cooperative. A cooperative, or co-op, is a type of business that is owned by the people who work in it, rather than by an individual owner. The co-op that Andrés and Daniel belong to employs 40 young people from the community. Through it, Andrés and the other young workers are learning how to run a business.

Andrés thinks the co-op is an exciting place to work, and he's become good friends with some of the other workers. Everyone shares equally in the work as well as in the money that they earn. At co-op meetings, everyone votes on how the business should be run. Now and then, of course, the group argues about how something should be done, but business generally runs smoothly. Sometimes, if they need advice, they call on adults from the church.

Top: Andrés designs and outlines the artwork on one of the crosses.
Bottom: An entire table full of young people adds bright-colored paint to the crosses. Some of the crosses carry Andrés' designs.

Andrés and Daniel do well in their jobs. Their earnings make them the family's top wage earners. Andrés works in the co-op for four hours each morning and then attends school for four hours in the afternoon. He spends much of his time at the co-op drawing and painting pictures. Together, Andrés and the other co-op workers create beautiful note cards, paintings, jewelry, needlework, Christmas cards, and hand-painted wooden crosses. They then ship these goods to churches in North America and Europe, where they are sold.

Andrés also works in the carpentry shop. Already he knows how to make several educational games and puzzles out of wood. Schools and day-care centers buy many of these. Lately, Daniel has been teaching Andrés how to use the workshop's electric table saw. Andrés is eager to learn because with this saw, he will be able to build furniture.

Products from the crafts co-op include note cards, Christmas cards, paintings, and wooden crosses.

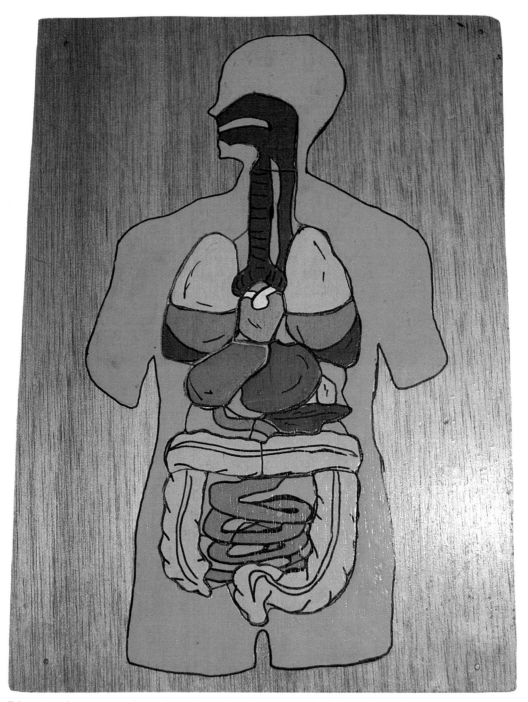

Educational games and puzzles sell well at the co-op. Andrés is pleased that with what he has learned in the carpentry shop, he can now create puzzles such as this one of the human body.

School Life in Oscar Romero

Andrés attends a Catholic elementary school from 1:30 to 5:30 each weekday afternoon. Other co-op workers also attend this school, which has 500 students. Andrés is in the fourth grade, where his teacher says that he is one of the hardest-working pupils. Andrés shrugs; he just wants to do well. With reading and social studies, it's easy because they are his favorite classes. With subjects such as math, science, and geography, he has to push himself harder.

In the refugee camp, Andrés did not attend a regular school. Volunteer teachers held classes, but the students far outnumbered the teachers. Even so, Andrés gratefully remembers their efforts. Through them he learned to paint and draw. Sometimes, when his studies frustrate him, he remembers how much he missed school when he was in the camp. Somehow, that makes the work seem a little easier.

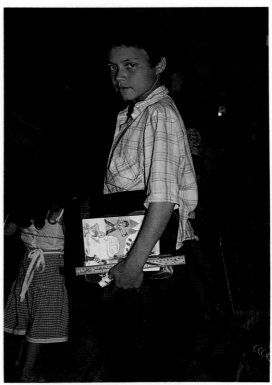

With an armful of books and supplies, Andrés heads out the door for school.

Above: Andrés and the other fourth-graders gather for a class photo in front of the Catholic elementary school in Oscar Romero. Not even the camera is quick enough to make everyone appear to be standing still.
Right: In a more serious moment, Andrés turns all of his attention to one of his books.

Recess at last! Laughing, running, and jumping, the fourth-graders release a morning's worth of energy.

The Oscar Romero neighborhood has only one public school, although the area includes 10,000 children of school age. Many of these children cannot go to school unless they can either attend one of the church-supported schools or afford to travel to school in another neighborhood. Only the three oldest Navarro boys attend school, although Dagoberta and Francisco took classes in the refugee camp. Often, a Salvadoran couple cannot afford to send all the children to school, so they send the oldest boys. Dagoberta, like other Salvadoran girls, rarely attends school because she must do essential family work.

The church also operates several neighborhood day-care centers. The centers care for the community's preschool children, allowing their parents to take jobs in the city. Some of the children at the centers are orphans. Thousands of Salvadoran children have lost one or both parents in the civil war. Although Andrés' family has had hard times, he thinks being an orphan would be worse than anything he has experienced.

Top: One of Andrés' pictures shows his class on a recent field trip.
Bottom: It may be nap time in this day-care center, but not everyone is sleepy.

25

Andrés' Favorite Things

After school and on weekends, Andrés has time for himself. Like many other Salvadorans, he is crazy about soccer. So he and his friends play nearly every day on a large, flat area near the railroad tracks in Oscar Romero. Andrés often plays the goalkeeper's position for his team. As goalie, Andrés defends his team's goal, or net, trying to keep the other team from kicking the ball past him.

When he's not on the soccer field, Andrés devotes time to his guitar. He began playing almost three years ago and has practiced nearly every day since. In the beginning, Andrés wondered if he could even learn to tune the guitar properly. He had almost given up when a teacher at school began giving him lessons. Now Andrés plays well, and his family and friends are always asking him to play for them. Everyone sings along when he plays their favorite songs.

Above: Andrés and his friends begin playing soccer the minute school lets out. They would probably play day and night if they could. Opposite: After a busy day of school and soccer, Andrés winds down with his guitar. ▶

Building a New Neighborhood

Andrés' family, like many other families in the neighborhood and throughout the country, has joined a housing cooperative. In this type of cooperative, people join together to buy land and build themselves decent houses. Churches often help cooperatives get started. They sometimes loan the families money to build their homes, and, in some cases, they buy the construction materials.

The housing cooperative that the Navarro family belongs to is called Apoyo Mutuo, which means "mutual aid." The 200 families that will live in the new community work together to clear the land and build the houses that they will own. Working side by side, the co-op members are forming strong friendships. The work is hard, and no one gets paid, but in two years the Navarros and the other families will get their reward — new houses and a good neighborhood.

Top: Because the co-op land covers a steep hill, workers must carve terraced lots into it. Here, the workers use a bulldozer to form the lots.
Bottom: Workers stand in the ditch in which a retaining wall will be built. This wall will secure the homes on the hill. The workers use tin cans filled with sand to pound down the earth before the wall is built.
Opposite: There's plenty of back-breaking work to be done before the houses will be complete. ▶

On weekends, the Navarros work at the site of their new house and neighborhood. Emilio sometimes works there during the week if he cannot find other jobs. Whenever he can, Andrés goes eagerly to the construction site to work beside his father, brothers, and the others. Working in the hot sun, hauling dirt in a wheelbarrow, or clearing stones, he knows he is helping his family. The thought of this pleases Andrés as he struggles to keep pace with the older men.

Andrés dreams of the day when the families will leave Oscar Romero's slums for the new neighborhood. He knows the Apoyo Mutuo houses will not be fancy, but they will have both electricity and running water. Best of all, the houses will be theirs. Andrés sees this as a chance to begin again. Sometimes at sunset, he walks to the construction site and to the spot where the Navarro house will stand. There, looking out over the city lit by the beautiful sunset colors, Andrés feels excitement run through him.

◀ Opposite: Even Andrés works at the site of their new home. He is proud that he can keep up with his brothers and his father.
Below: A view of the terraced hill. Houses will be built on each flat step of the hillside.

To Market, to Market

Catalina and Dagoberta do most of the family's food shopping. Andrés and some of the younger children, who consider shopping more fun than work, always offer to help. For much of their food, the family shops either in the neighborhood market or in San Salvador's central market, which is 15 minutes away by bus. The local market is easy to get to, but Catalina finds that food is often cheaper at the downtown market.

Andrés eagerly awaits the occasional trips to San Salvador's central market. This market sprawls with hundreds of stalls selling everything from food and clothing to school supplies and books. Andrés and the other children never tire of watching the different people bustle about the market. They could stay and watch them for hours. Until they moved to San Salvador, the Navarro children had never seen such a huge market.

San Salvador's central market can offer a greater variety of products than the neighborhood market can. There, food and other basic items are surrounded by clothes, books, toys, and all sorts of electronic items that catch the children's attention.

But Andrés considers even a trip to the neighborhood market an adventure. To get there, he climbs the hill overlooking the soccer field and walks along the railroad tracks. Trains run along these tracks three or four times a day, and Andrés often meets one on his way. As the train zooms by, he waves to the train conductor riding in the caboose. Sometimes he meets vendors selling their goods at the houses that line the tracks and walks with them awhile.

The local market is also a place to meet friends. The vendors know most of their customers by name, so shopping is a time to visit as well as to buy. Nearly every trip, the family buys staple foods such as rice, red beans, and corn tortillas. They eat these foods every day. Their diet also includes bananas, eggs, and chicken, but these they buy less often. On special occasions, Catalina sends Andrés to the market for fresh fish, his favorite food. On those trips, he rarely dawdles.

Left: Even the quiet neighborhood market offers plenty of sights, sounds, and smells. Opposite: The smell from the market's fresh fish supply always catches Andrés' nose. Opposite, inset: "Fish today, Andrés?" a smiling vendor calls out.

Andrés Makes a Kite

Kite flying has grown popular among young people in El Salvador. Since Andrés, like most children in Oscar Romero, doesn't have much money to spend, he has learned how to make his own kite. First, he finds a dried cornstalk that is long enough to form the kite's frame. Using a sharp knife called a machete, he slices the cornstalk lengthwise into two thin rods. Next, he takes a plastic bag and cuts it to make the kite's sail. He then measures the rods to fit the plastic sail.

Now that he has all the pieces, Andrés puts the kite together. With string, he fastens the sail to the ends and center of the rods. He uses small pieces of tape to help secure the kite. He then trims the edges of the plastic. At last, Andrés adds a long, thin piece of cloth for a tail. The tail will give the kite balance. Now the kite is ready to fly, and Andrés heads for the street.

Top: With his father's machete, Andrés slices the cornstalk to make the kite frame.
Bottom: Andrés cuts the kite's lower edges to give it balance.
Opposite: When the wind is too weak to fly the kite in the street, Catalina allows Andrés to fly it from the roof of the house. ▶

Sundays: A Time for Rest and Recreation

Andrés looks forward to Sunday afternoons all week. The family sets this afternoon aside specifically for free time. The afternoon usually begins with everyone gathering for lunch. Then, after lunch, everyone spends the day as he or she chooses. Today, Andrés plays guitar and sings songs for the family and several visitors. Daniel jokingly tells him that he should forget painting and become a pop singer.

Later, Andrés suggests that everyone dance. He turns on the radio, searching for a catchy folk song, some rock 'n' roll, or a Latin tune. When a North American rock 'n' roll tune catches his ear, he turns it up loud. The Navarros are known to be good dancers. Even the youngest children dance well. Every month, the neighborhood holds street dances. Although Andrés looks forward to the dances, he is always shy about asking the girls to dance.

Top: A pot of beans simmers on an open fire.
Bottom: With 11 family members, there aren't enough chairs for everyone to sit at once. So the family eats in shifts. Here, some of the younger children hungrily eat their lunch of beans and tortillas.

Above: The younger Navarro children learned to dance by watching the older ones. Here, Andrés' younger brothers practice some of the new steps that Rafael and Daniel have shown them. Before long, everyone will be dancing. Right: Francisco and Marcos show off some of the family's animals. Francisco holds their pet puppy; Marcos holds one of their chickens.

A slight mist hangs over Lake Ilopango. This lake is a favorite weekend spot for many Salvadorans.

A Trip to Lake Ilopango

For a special outing this Sunday, the Navarro family takes the bus to Lake Ilopango for a picnic. Ilopango, located 10 miles (16 km) from San Salvador, fills an old volcano crater. The entire family is anxious to get to the lake because hot, sticky weather has enveloped the town for days. Everyone hopes to feel the lake's cool breezes soon.

Catalina packs a huge lunch of rice, beans, tortillas, and bananas. At the lake, Andrés eats hungrily, nodding in agreement when Emilio says that food tastes better on a picnic. After lunch, while the adults walk along the lakeshore, the children race off for a swim. Andrés, Francisco, Rafael, and Daniel leave the water to climb the steep bluffs overlooking the lake. As Andrés stretches out atop one bluff to watch the white-capped waves break on the shore below, he wishes all of life were as peaceful as this moment.

Taking a break from the beach, Andrés, Francisco, Mario, and Marcos treat themselves to a soda at a nearby refreshment stand.

Emilio surprises everyone with a boat ride on the lake. Many of the children have not been on a boat before this. After seeing the white-capped waves from the cliffs above, Andrés knows the ride will be a bumpy one.

Sunday Mass

On Sunday evenings, the family attends church services. Two priests serve the Catholic community: Father Pablo and Father Camilio. In his sermon tonight, Father Pablo reminds the parishioners that Jesus chose to live and work as a carpenter among the poor. He compares Jesus' work to the work of the people in Apoyo Mutuo and encourages the people to be proud of their work. Listening to Father Pablo's words, Andrés feels good inside.

As Mass ends, the people shake hands or hug as a sign of peace. Andrés notices that everyone is still smiling as they leave church. He wonders if Father Pablo's words have made everyone feel as good as they make him feel. He realizes how important the priests are to him and the community. They not only conduct the Mass but also have worked hard to establish the schools, the day-care centers, and the cooperatives.

Above: A North American priest who works in Oscar Romero's Catholic community stops before Mass to talk to one of the young parishioners.
Opposite: As Mass ends, everyone offers each other a sign of peace. Mario is just the right size for one of Maria's hugs. ▶

A Message of Peace to the World

This week, Andrés and his family attend a peace march in San Salvador. Organized by the churches, the march attracts over 25,000 people, including many children. To see so many people marching for peace gives Andrés hope. Perhaps by the time he's ready for high school, a peace treaty will have ended the civil war. He hopes so. In the meantime, he's glad to be surrounded by his family and friends, studying and working for a better tomorrow.

After the march, Andrés draws a greeting card for the children of the world. In Spanish, the card says: "We Salvadorans wish you the best. In your countries or states, we hope that we find you well. Here what we like to do is study, work, play ball and marbles, and fly kites. We all go to the playground every day at San Patricio School. My name is Andrés Navarro Aquino. I know many animals: deer, birds, cows, donkeys, dogs, cats. My brothers, sisters, and I send greetings to all children."

Top: People in the march carry banners and palm fronds decorated with paper flowers.
Bottom: Workers organize the order in which the many banners will be carried in the march.

No sotros las salvadorenos les deseamas que les baya muy bien en los estados en peramos que se encuentren bien nosotros aqui lo que los guta es estudiar trabajar los gusta jugar pelota piscucha chivola bamos ala camcha ajugar todos los de la Escuela San Patricio. yo me yamo Andrés Navarro Aquino Conosco muchas animales el venado las aves las Jacas burro perro gato y mis Hermanitos Saludes atodos los niñes

Sansalvador CA

A message of peace from Andrés.

FOR YOUR INFORMATION: El Salvador

Official Name: República de El Salvador
(ray-POOH-blee-kah deh el SAL-vah-dore)
Republic of El Salvador

Capital: San Salvador

History

The Pipil Indian Civilization of El Salvador

Pipil and Maya Indians were among the first inhabitants of what is now El Salvador. The Pipil natives, who were related to the Aztec Indians of Mexico, came to dominate the area in the eleventh century. They called the land Cuscatlán, which means "land of beautiful things." As the Pipil villages took control of the territory, many of the original Maya tribes left El Salvador, migrating north to Guatemala and Mexico.

Salvadorans load barrels of water onto their ox carts. Ox carts like these are used for hauling in many rural areas of El Salvador.

The Pipil lived mainly by farming. Although corn became their most important crop, they also raised bees for honey and cultivated beans, peppers, squash, cocoa, cotton, and tobacco. Once settled in this agricultural lifestyle, the Pipil built a distinct culture. They excelled at weaving, pottery making, carpentry, and masonry. They developed systems of writing and mathematics. They also established a monetary system using cocoa plant seeds as money.

The ruins of Pipil temples and villages stand throughout El Salvador. Direct descendants of the Pipil tribes still inhabit rural villages such as Panchimalco, which is located south of San Salvador, the capital city. The Indians living there, known as the Panchos, comprise one of the last full-blooded Indian groups in El Salvador. Many of these Indians continue their ancestors' ways, speaking their native language of Nahuatl, as well as practicing traditional dances and religious ceremonies.

The Spanish Conquest in El Salvador, 1524-1821

The Spanish conquistadores first invaded Cuscatlán in 1524. With visions of more land and gold before them, the Spaniards had spread southward from newly conquered territories in Mexico. The Indians of Cuscatlán resisted the Spaniards, who were led by Pedro de Alvarado, and drove them from the area. Alvarado and his men returned a year later, and after almost three years of fighting, they managed to subdue the Pipils in 1528.

Even after the Spanish victory, many Indians refused to accept Alvarado's authority and fled into remote areas. The Spaniards forced the remaining Indians to work for them. Under a system called the *encomienda*, Spain awarded huge tracts of land and the Indians needed to work them to certain colonists in the new territories. According to the Spanish law of the encomienda, the Indians had to work for the landowners. In return, the landowners were to protect and take care of their Indian subjects. In reality, the Spaniards treated the Pipils as slaves. The landowners forced the natives to pay them tribute, or taxes, in the form of most of the crops they raised. The Spaniards tortured or killed the Pipils who resisted.

Over the centuries, the Spanish and Indian bloodlines mixed. Children of these intermarriages are called *mestizos*, and they soon became a large sector of the population. Slowly, and often painfully, the two cultures began to blend, as many mestizos adopted Spanish customs. But Spain was too busy with some of its other New World colonies to notice. Because El Salvador did not have the large gold and silver deposits that the conquistadores had hoped for, Spain paid little attention to the quiet colony until the 1800s.

Independence from Spain and the Rise of "King Coffee"

In 1821, Spain became more aware of all of its Central American colonies.
On September 15 of that year, the colonies, which included Costa Rica,
Guatemala, Honduras, Nicaragua, and El Salvador, demanded and gained
their independence. Almost at once, Agustín de Iturbide, the self-proclaimed
emperor of Mexico (which had also broken from Spain), tried to add the
colonies to his new empire. Only El Salvador resisted. But before Iturbide
could force that province into the empire, revolution in Mexico toppled his
government in 1823. The five Central American provinces once again
proclaimed their independence, and shortly after united as the Central
American Federation. When this federation finally fell apart in late 1840,
El Salvador and the other federation members rose as independent nations.

In the late 19th century, landowners on El Salvador's plantations, or *fincas*,
began to grow coffee. The country's volcanic soil and its warm, damp climate
proved ideal for the coffee plant. Cotton growing also became profitable.
As the demand for these crops grew, the landowners wanted more land.
They began to buy or take over any available fertile land, often pushing Indian
farmers off their small plots of corn and beans. After losing their land, these
small farmers had no means of support. Many had to go to work as coffee
pickers on the very plantations that had swallowed their land.

The Rise of the Military Dictators

For a short time in the early 1900s, the country entered a period of stability.
At this time, a small group of rich plantation owners grew very powerful. These
landowners, known as the Catorce Familias, or the "fourteen families," controlled El Salvador's government. One landowner after another held a term as
president as a means of protecting their interests. This orderly process created a
more stable government that encouraged economic growth while allowing
poor living conditions to continue for most of El Salvador's people.

But this system could not withstand the problems that hit the country's economy
when worldwide coffee and cotton prices fell drastically in 1929. Plantation
owners could no longer find buyers for their coffee and cotton. As production
on the plantations slowed, the peasants who depended on this work grew des-
perate. Rather than watch their families starve, the peasants organized themselves to take back some of the lands that the plantation owners had taken
from them. A rebellion erupted, led by Farabundo Martí.

In putting down the rebellion, General Maximiliano Hernández Martinez seized
power in El Salvador in 1931. Under his command, the military carried out *la
matanza*, or "the Great Massacre." Hernández put the number murdered at

8,000; others claim it was closer to 30,000. The majority of those killed were Pancho Indians. Hernández's brutal rule lasted until 1944, when a revolution of soldiers and students overthrew him. Since then, military leaders have frequently held power in El Salvador.

Current History

A bloody civil war fought between government and rebel troops has raged in El Salvador since the late 1970s. A group called the Farabundo Martí Front for National Liberation (FMLN) leads the rebel forces. According to these rebels, the country's wealthy class refuses to share wealth or political power with the poor, who make up 80% of the population. However, those who support the present government say that the rebels are dictatorial communists who wish to take over the lands and businesses of the upper class for their own benefit. Since the civil war began, over 75,000 people have been killed, most of them civilians killed by the army or death squads. Another 1.5 million people (about 25% of the total population) have been displaced from their homes.

In 1979, protests broke out in force. People demanded that the government pay attention to the needs of the poor masses. In October of that year, civilians and military officers interested in reform overthrew the existing government, removing then president Carlos Humberto Romero from office. A *junta*, or ruling council, composed of three civilians and two military officers replaced Romero, hoping to bring reforms that would quell the violence. This was not to be. Violence, including kidnappings and assassinations, became common on both the rebel and government sides. In 1980, Archbishop Oscar Arnulfo Romero y Galdames, who had gained popularity as an open, influential critic of the government, was assassinated. Archbishop Romero's death ignited protests and demonstrations throughout the country.

Until 1984, this combined military and civilian government controlled El Salvador with José Napoleón Duarte appointed as leader. Since this period, the United States has given substantial military and economic aid to El Salvador, urging the government to end its violence and to promote modest land reform. The government has since begun a land redistribution program, but it has not had much success, and El Salvador is still a nation marked by violence. The government has also taken control of, or nationalized, banking and other industries to stimulate the economy. By 1983, a Constituent Assembly had rewritten the country's constitution to call for nationwide presidential elections. The elections officially named Duarte to a five-year term as president.

In 1989, Duarte's party was replaced by the Nationalist Republic Alliance (ARENA) as El Salvador's ruling party. The FMLN and many opposition forces refused to participate in the elections that put ARENA in power. They stated that free elections were impossible without a cease-fire and an end to the military control of the country. Many Salvadorans doubt the new government's ability to help the economy or save the country from the corruption that plagues it. Other people believe that ARENA is linked to the death squads that have kidnapped and murdered thousands of Salvadorans who have opposed the government. Church and opposition leaders have specifically accused Roberto D'Aubuisson, ARENA's founder and leader, of ordering Archbishop Romero's assassination in 1980. ARENA claims that it no longer has ties to death-squad activities.

As the civil war has continued through the 1980s and into the 1990s, church and peace groups have called for a cutoff of US military aid to the Salvadoran armed forces and for the signing of a peace treaty between the FMLN and the government. The two sides did begin peace talks in late 1989. Representatives gathered in San José, Costa Rica, with President Oscar Arias Sánchez of Costa Rica mediating. Discussions lasted three days, but the opposing sides reached no agreements other than the agreement to meet again. Since then, rebel forces have broken off negotiations, and the fighting continues.

Government

El Salvador's government functions under a constitution written in 1983. This constitution declares the country a republic and calls for three branches of government: executive, legislative, and judicial. The constitution also divides the country into 14 departments, or states. Each of these departments has a governor, appointed by the president.

The 1983 constitution states that the president heads the government. It also specifies that each president is elected by popular vote and serves a five-year term. In the past, the control that the military and ruling class exerted over the government often included choosing the president. Since the 1930s, in fact, most of the country's leaders have come from within the military. Presidents or other officials who opposed the military often held office for only a short time.

El Salvador's legislative body, the National Assembly, consists of 60 representatives who are elected by popular vote to serve three-year terms. The number of representatives, or deputies, from each department varies according to its population. Aside from its law-making duties, the assembly must appoint 14 judges to the supreme court — El Salvador's highest judicial body.

City and town councils provide local government, but these elected bodies have very little power in comparison to the national government or even the army. The army (with about 55,000 soldiers) has forts and barracks in most cities and towns. From its posts, the military keeps a close watch on people's activities. The army claims that such surveillance helps it fight terrorism.

Language

Spanish is the official language of the country, although the people in certain Indian communities speak their native languages. Indian organizations encourage the study of their native languages to preserve their cultural heritage. English remains the most widely studied second language in the schools.

Land and Climate

El Salvador ranks as Central America's smallest country. It covers 8,260 square miles (21,390 sq km) of land, which is almost four times the size of the Canadian province of Prince Edward Island, but compares in size to the US state of Massachusetts. To the north and east of El Salvador lies Honduras, and to the west lies Guatemala. The Pacific Ocean forms the country's southern border.

A mountainous highland, the country's most distinctive feature, cuts through the middle of El Salvador, running northwest to southeast. Volcanoes dot the area. The highest of them, called Santa Ana, stands 7,830 feet (2,390 m) above sea level. Because of the volcanoes, eruptions and earthquakes remain a constant threat. Although volcanic activity has played a constant role in El Salvador's history, none of the volcanoes has erupted since 1976.

The remainder of El Salvador's land area falls into two distinct regions: the central plateau and the coastal lowlands. South of the volcanic range lies the central plateau, interrupted in places by mountains that drop steeply into the Pacific Ocean. The majority of El Salvador's population lives on this plateau, with its rich volcanic soil. Farmers use about 80% of the most fertile land exclusively for growing coffee. The coastal region borders the central plateau to the south. This area runs the length of the country against the Pacific Ocean but extends only 10 to 20 miles (16 to 32 km) inward. Fertile soil also covers this area, and the large plantations, or fincas, employ much of the land.

The country has a tropical climate that cools slightly toward the mountainous areas. Except in the highest elevations, temperatures range from 73°-80°F (23°-27°C). Temperatures peak in the months of March, April, and May; December, January, and February record the coolest temperatures. Rain falls heavily throughout the country from May to October, when moist winds blow in from the Pacific Ocean. During the rest of the year, it rarely rains at all. The country receives an average of about 72 inches (1,830 mm) of rain per year.

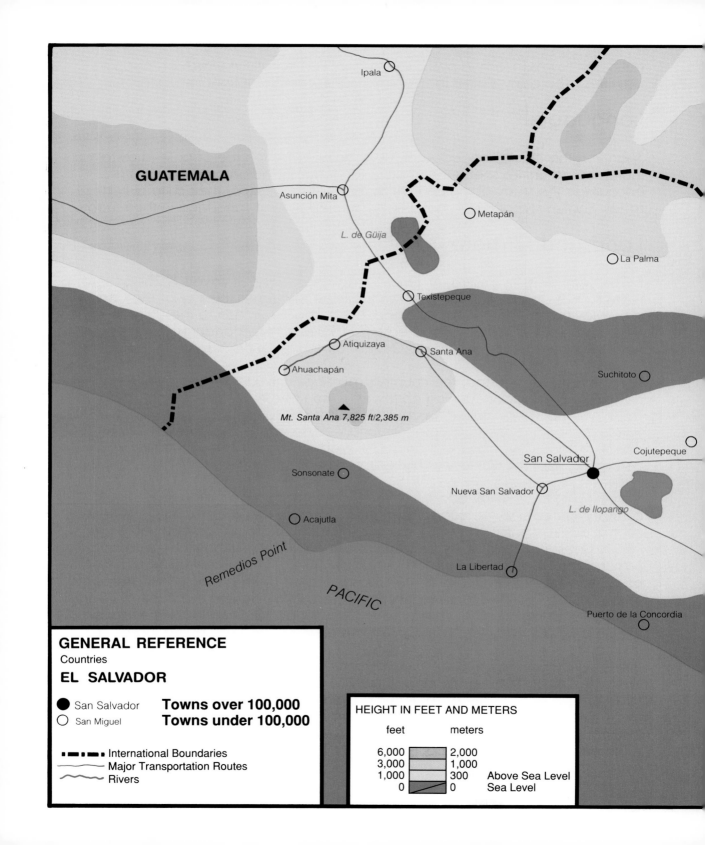

GUATEMALA

Ipala

Asunción Mita

L. de Güija

Metapán

La Palma

Texistepeque

Atiquizaya

Santa Ana

Suchitoto

Ahuachapán

▲
Mt. Santa Ana 7,825 ft/2,385 m

Cojutepeque

San Salvador

Sonsonate

Nueva San Salvador

L. de Ilopango

Acajutla

Remedios Point

La Libertad

PACIFIC

Puerto de la Concordia

GENERAL REFERENCE
Countries
EL SALVADOR

● San Salvador   **Towns over 100,000**
○ San Miguel   **Towns under 100,000**

▄▪▄▪▄ International Boundaries
⎯ Major Transportation Routes
⎯ Rivers

HEIGHT IN FEET AND METERS

feet   meters

6,000   2,000
3,000   1,000
1,000   300   Above Sea Level
   0   0   Sea Level

EL SALVADOR — Political and Physical

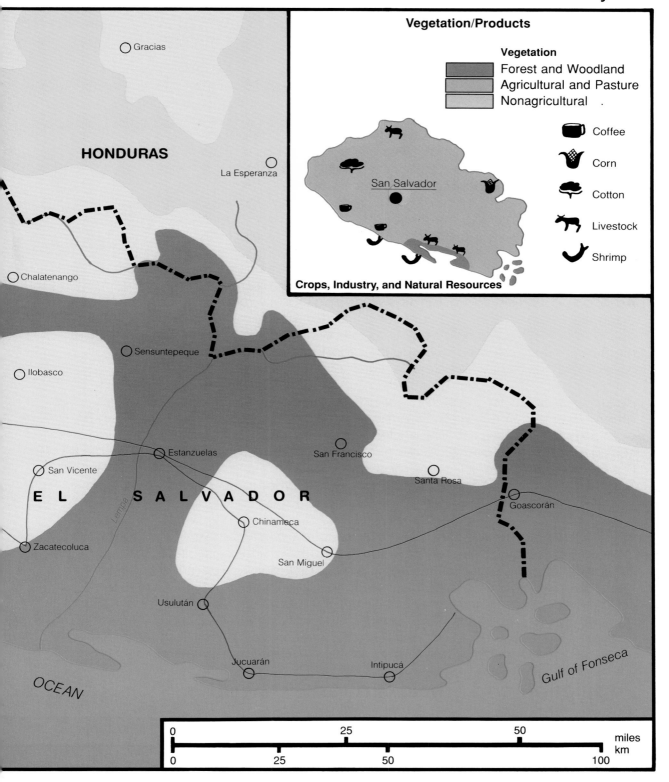

Vegetation/Products

Vegetation
- Forest and Woodland
- Agricultural and Pasture
- Nonagricultural

- Coffee
- Corn
- Cotton
- Livestock
- Shrimp

San Salvador

Crops, Industry, and Natural Resources

Gracias

HONDURAS

La Esperanza

Chalatenango

Sensuntepeque

Ilobasco

Estanzuelas

San Vicente

E L   S A L V A D O R

San Francisco

Santa Rosa

Goascorán

Zacatecoluca

Lempa

Chinameca

San Miguel

Usulután

Jucuarán

Intipucá

Gulf of Fonseca

OCEAN

| 0 | | 25 | | 50 | | miles |
| 0 | 25 | 50 | | | 100 | km |

Natural Resources, Agriculture, and Industry

Given its mild climate and natural resources, El Salvador has the potential to be a prosperous country. Its fertile volcanic soil ranks as its chief resource. Other leading natural resources include a developing fishing industry off the Pacific coast and limited deposits of gold and silver. Forests produce such trees as oak, cedar, and mahogany. Long ago, these valuable trees blanketed the country. But the expanding production of crops for export has reduced the forests until they now cover only about 6% of the land — one of the lowest percentages of forest land in Latin America. Hydroelectric power (electric power generated by rivers) and geothermal power (heat generated by underground volcanic springs) are also among the major resources. Hydroelectric plants on the Lempa River already produce most of the country's electricity.

Because of its rich soil, El Salvador's economy revolves around agriculture. About 40% of the nation's labor force works in farming. As in many Central American countries, many farmers work small family farms where they raise staple crops, such as corn, beans, and rice, for their families and for the local markets. Owners of the huge plantations control most of the fertile land in the highlands. Because they own the best land, these farmers also grow and control most of the export crops, such as coffee, cotton, and sugarcane.

Recently, El Salvador's government has encouraged growth in the country's other industries. The government believes that stronger industries will keep the economy from being too dependent on agriculture. Main industries include chemicals, textiles, food processing, tobacco products, and petroleum products. But the sale of coffee still earns most of the country's export income. The United States buys 48% of El Salvador's exports, while other large customers include West Germany (21%), Guatemala (9%), and Japan (5%).

In El Salvador, a small portion of the population controls most of the national income. Generally, people in this small group own the agricultural land and the industries. This situation creates a distinct division between rich and poor. In El Salvador, about 80% of the population lives in poverty. Overall, unemployment or underemployment (lack of full-time employment) affects 50% of the population. Currently, US economic and military aid and money from Salvadorans living outside the country keep the economy afloat. Money sent in by these refugees supports close to 40% of the families inside the country.

Population and Ethnic Groups

El Salvador's population totals approximately 5.5 million people. The majority of these people live in rural areas and depend on agriculture for their livelihood. The largest city in the country is San Salvador, with an estimated area population of over one million people. The next largest urban area is Santa Ana (population 416,880), followed by San Miguel (population 112,600) and Santa Tecia (population 52,560).

The country ranks as Central America's most densely populated country, with about 666 persons per square mile (257 persons per sq km). The population continues to grow at approximately 3% per year. At this rapid rate, El Salvador's population grows five times faster than that of the United States.

Mestizos, or people of mixed Spanish and Indian heritage, make up over 90% of the country's population. Full-blooded Indians account for only 5% to 7%, and another 2% of the people claim to be full-blooded Europeans.

Education

In El Salvador, the law requires children between the ages of 7 and 12 years to attend school. Government funds support the school system, but this funding does not meet the nation's educational needs, especially in the rural areas. The school system suffers shortages of everything from books and supplies to classrooms and teachers. To make up for this lack, some of the country's churches build and run their own schools. But even this effort is not enough. Over 30% of El Salvador's children currently do not attend school.

Students who complete the six years of primary school may go on to a secondary school and eventually even a university. But the percentage of students attending and graduating decreases greatly at each higher level. Approximately 65,000 Salvadorans now attend the country's universities. Unfortunately, education suffers at all levels in El Salvador. The severity of the problem shows in the fact that over 40% of the total population can neither read nor write.

Religion

Approximately 85% of El Salvador's population practices Roman Catholicism. An archbishop in San Salvador and bishops in four other cities, as well as local parish priests, serve this large Catholic community. Most other Salvadorans who practice an organized religion are Protestants or Jews.

Many groups, such as the Catholic, Lutheran, Episcopalian, and Baptist churches, have taken active roles in the civil rights and political struggles of the country. Some have established programs to help victims of the fighting. Others, like Archbishop Romero, have spoken out against the brutality or have demanded that the army and the rebels sign a peace treaty to end the civil war.

Arts and Crafts

As is true of many Central American countries that once belonged to the Spanish Empire, El Salvador's cultural life shows a blend of both Indian and Spanish elements. But in recent years, El Salvador's cultural life has become less distinctive. This is due in part to US and European influence. Salvadoran youth, especially in the capital and other large cities, follows US and European music, dance, and art. In rural areas, particularly in the Indian villages, tradition still dominates. But to a greater extent, both the military government, which has held power since the 1970s, and the ongoing civil war have suppressed cultural growth. Both the government and the war have made it difficult for artists to continue their traditional work or to expand into new art styles.

Characteristics of traditional Salvadoran culture can still be seen in the native handicraft that is produced throughout the country. Artisans produce bright-colored textiles, sisal (hemp) hammocks, pottery, leather goods, and painted wood carvings. To produce these items, Salvadorans often rely on techniques begun by their ancestors. Weaving, for example, calls for the same kind of hand or foot loom that people have used for centuries.

So many Salvadorans excel at weaving, and the craft has become so specialized, that certain villages and cities produce only certain products, such as hammocks, mats, or hats. This is similar to specialized weaving in Guatemala, El Salvador's northwestern neighbor. While in El Salvador the *product* woven tells something of its origin, in Guatemala the *pattern* of the weaving reveals this information. Some artisans now combine ancient techniques with modern products, producing beach towels, T-shirts, kitchen utensils, and other souvenirs. But whether the techniques and products are traditional or modern, many families rely heavily on these crafts to make a living.

Sports and Entertainment

In El Salvador, as in many other Latin American countries, soccer is a national passion. In El Salvador, it is also the national sport. Salvadorans of all ages regularly play soccer and form teams — in the neighborhood, at school, and especially at the high school and university level. Players at the university level often compete for positions on the national soccer team, which plays in international matches.

Salvadorans also play basketball, swim, box, wrestle, and bicycle. Since many people are poor, the most popular Salvadoran sports don't require special equipment. Sports that do require more specialized equipment, such as boating, golf, bowling, and tennis, have gained popularity among middle-class people.

Currency

The *colón*, named for Cristóbal Colón (Christopher Columbus), serves as the basic unit of money in El Salvador. At 1989 rates, 5.5 colones equals one US dollar. One colón also equals 100 Salvadoran *centavos*.

Salvadoran paper money and coins. The art on the bills honors El Salvador's history.

San Salvador

The Spanish colonists established San Salvador, which means "Holy Savior," in 1525. A year later, an earthquake destroyed most of the original city. Two moves brought San Salvador to its present location in 1545. But even this location has not been a peaceful spot. Major earthquakes hit the city in 1854, 1917, and most recently in 1986, causing extensive damage each time.

What remains of the capital city's colonial-style buildings stand near the city's center. Two of these buildings, the National Palace, built in 1904, and the Teatro Nacional (National Theater) present fine examples of traditional colonial architecture. The National Palace serves as headquarters for the National Assembly. The Parque Libertad, a park just across the street, is often the site of meetings and rallies. The palace and the park together keep the area full of people and hot with political activity. Not far away is the restored church of La Merced, where rebels launched the 1811 movement for independence from Spain. Today, San Salvador is the largest city in the country. Over the last ten years, migrating war refugees have swelled the population to an estimated one million people. This means that almost one-fifth of El Salvador's total population lives in the capital city area. The city cannot keep up with this growth. Employment and housing have fallen far short of the city's needs, and many people live in the poverty-stricken slums that fringe the city.

Salvadorans in North America

According to varying estimates, El Salvador's civil war and failing economy have driven between 500,000 and one million Salvadorans from their country. Many of these people have resettled in neighboring Central American countries, Mexico, the United States, and Canada. Because many refugees have entered North America illegally, government officials cannot determine their exact numbers.

The majority of these Salvadorans say that they are political refugees, fleeing government violence and political repression. Even so, US immigration officials have refused 95% of the requests for political asylum. The immigration officials claim that most Salvadorans come to the United States to find jobs, not to escape political repression.

Partially as a result of these immigration policies, over 300 US churches and synagogues have declared themselves sanctuaries for Salvadoran and Guatemalan refugees. Religious sanctuary groups have helped thousands of refugees enter the United States through an underground railroad. This system takes its name from the 19th-century Underground Railroad in the United States. Through the original Underground Railroad, opponents of slavery helped slaves escape to freedom. In that tradition, modern churches aid Central American refugees in their escape from their war-torn countries. In some cases, the US government has jailed church activists for their actions.

More Books about El Salvador

El Salvador: Beauty among the Ashes. Adams (Dillon Press)
El Salvador: Country in Crisis. Cheney (Franklin Watts)
El Salvador in Pictures. Lerner Publications Dept. of Geography Staff (Lerner)
Enchantment of Central America: El Salvador. Carpenter and Baker
    (Childrens Press)
Fire from the Sky. Vornberger, editor (Writers and Readers Publishing
    Cooperative)

Glossary of Useful Salvadoran (Spanish) Terms

adobe (ah-DOH-be) .... bricks made out of sun-dried mud
Apoyo Mutuo (ah-POY-oh mu-TWO-oh) .... mutual aid or cooperation
barrio (bah-REE-oh) .... a neighborhood, usually a poor one
colón (koh-LONE) .... the monetary unit of El Salvador
colonia (koh-LOH-nya) .... a neighborhood in a city
conquistadores (kohn-kees-tuh-DOOR-rays) .. "conquerors"; Spanish soldiers
Cuscatlán (koos-kaht-LAHN) .... Pipil name for El Salvador
encomienda (en-kome-ee-EN-duh) .... system of semi-slavery
machete (mah-CHEH-teh) .... a large, heavy knife
mestizos (mess-TEE-sohs) .... people of Indian-Spanish blood
molino (moh-LEE-noh) .... a machine that grinds corn

Pipil (PEE-peel) ....the original natives of El Salvador
tortilla (tor-TEE-uh).....................................a thin crepelike corn bread

Things to Do — Research Projects

El Salvador's history, like that of many Central American countries, has been marked by political struggle and injustice and brutality from its ruling groups — conditions that plague it even today. El Salvador's problems are multiplied by its poor economic condition and its rapidly growing population. As you read more about this country, you will need current facts. Some of the research projects that follow will also require accurate, up-to-date information from current sources. Two publications that your library may have will tell you about recent newspaper and magazine articles on many topics:

Readers' Guide to Periodical Literature
Children's Magazine Guide

For accurate answers to questions about such topics as El Salvador's political situation, look up *El Salvador* in these publications. They will lead you to up-to-date information.

1. In the early 20th century, 14 families, known as the Catorce Familias, dominated El Salvador. These families — already wealthy from their plantations — grew powerful in the country's politics. Find out more about this ruling class. How did their actions affect the country?

2. Government troops and rebel forces (primarily the FMLN) represent the two sides of El Salvador's civil war. Articles about the civil war and these opposing groups have appeared regularly in recent newspapers and magazines. Find and read enough of these articles to write a brief description of the situation.

3. Learn what you can about the 19th-century US movement known as the Underground Railroad. Also see what you can find out about the more recent sanctuary movement. How do the two movements compare? How are they different?

More Things to Do — Activities

These projects are designed to encourage you to think more about El Salvador. They offer ideas for interesting group or individual projects for school or home.

1. Andrés lives in a simple house. Compare your home with his. How are they alike? How are they different? To better understand Andrés' life, talk with your parents, grandparents, or someone else whose early homes may not have had modern conveniences.

2. Moving can be hard. Talk with someone who has moved from the country to the city or from the city to the country. How does that person feel about the move? How do his or her feelings and comments compare with those of Andrés? How would you feel about such a move?

3. How far is El Salvador from wherever you live? Examine El Salvador's geography on a map of Central America. Find San Salvador and Lake Ilopango. Find out the total land area of your country and compare it to that of El Salvador. If you look up the population of your country, you could even compare the population densities of the two countries.

4. If you would like a pen pal in El Salvador, write to either of these two groups:

International Pen Friends
P.O. Box 290065
Brooklyn, NY 11229

Worldwide Pen Friends
P.O. Box 39097
Downey, CA 90241

Be sure to tell them what country you want your pen pal to be from. Also include your full name, age, and address.

Andrés wishes a bright future for all the children of the world.

Index